Something to Think About

Something to Think About

―――――

Figuring Out What's Important

and

Learning How to Defend It

By:

Aunt Kimmie Bebo

Edited by:

Mimi Dunham

ISBN: 150874887X
ISBN 13: 9781508748878
Library of Congress Control Number: 2015904190
Createspace Independent Publishing Platform
North Charleston, South Carolina

PRAISE FOR SOMETHING TO THINK ABOUT

I found myself looking forward to what great piece of advice would come next.
-Kaity Bailey, Heading out into the World

This book has a lot of insight about stuff teens are going through and about different parts of life that lay ahead.
-Gabrielle Saccomanno, High School Senior

These sparsely populated pages are packed with huge thoughts! It reads like a great conversation about what's really important.
-Traci Smith, Entrepreneur

This is writing from the heart that should be shared to encourage, strengthen, guide and inspire the younger ones in our midst.
–Anne Joyce, Registered Nurse and Full-time Mom

I thoroughly enjoy the dynamic advice Aunt Kimmie has to offer in this book! I will refer to it often!
-Piper Pillar, High School Sophomore

This is a great book filled with really good advice.
-Sonrisa Louise, 7th Grade

I am the richest person I know for having had in my life the
gracious influence of two exceptional women.
This book is dedicated to
the memory of my mom, Louise Bebo,
and
written in honor of my friend, Kimberly Dunham.

The author, age 13, with her mom – Spring 1983

A very special thanks to:

JOAN REDMAN
For suggesting the cover design for this book

LOU MAXEY
For her grammatical expertise

MY MANY AUNTIES (Barbara, Dian, Diane, Kathy, Mary, Patty)
For showing me the way

MY WONDERFUL HUSBAND
For all of his help, advice, love and support.

Dear Reader,

The inspiration for these words came from a letter I wrote to my niece for her 10th birthday. I wanted to give her something more lasting than a gift that would quickly be forgotten. I decided I wanted to give her something to think about.

I wrote the original letter by hand with an ink pen and good old-fashioned paper. I did that instead of typing, texting or emailing it, because it is so much more meaningful and personal to receive a handwritten letter. It always has been and it will always be. It makes me very sad that hardly anyone (including myself) ever takes the time to write a handwritten letter to the people they care about, appreciate and love.

My dear friend and mentor wanted a copy of the letter to give to her nieces for their high school graduation. One thing led to another, and Mimi Dunham and I revised and revisited the content so it would be more useful to three beautiful women embarking on their lives ... we ended-up with this book.

The following pages are everything I know and a bunch of stuff I'm still trying to learn. The topics are in no particular order so you don't need to read it beginning to end. It was written so you could just open it to a random page and have a little something to think about.

Whether you are 13 or 30, I send you my best wishes for a wondrous future and a remarkable life!

With Kind Consideration,

Aunt Kimmie

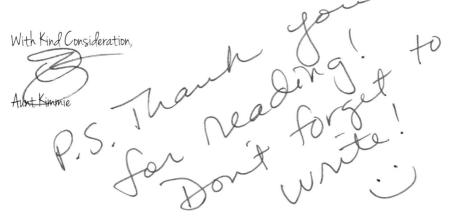

P.S. Thank you for Reading! Don't forget to write! :)

THE MOST REVERED WOMEN IN HISTORY DIDN'T EVEN ENTER THE CONTEST

Do not go where the path may lead, go instead where there is no path and leave a trail.

-Ralph Waldo Emerson

The most important thing to think about when considering popularity and good self-image is conviction. If you do nothing else in life, pick a few things to stand for. Beliefs, if you will, that you do not compromise for any reason. Beliefs that help you to make good decisions and guide you throughout your life.

THE STANDARD BY WHICH YOU LIVE.

For example, maybe you decide that you're going to be kind and gracious to everyone. If this is one of your standards, then you would choose not to associate with anyone who didn't treat others accordingly (think about the mean girls you know).

Even if it means not hanging out with "the popular girls."

When you've decided what you will stand for, you will not tolerate behavior that is not in keeping with your beliefs.

Your convictions will have already decided for you.

It may not be the popular decision – but it will be the right decision.

When you do things like this, you're sticking by your principles and you can't go wrong. There's no good that can come from associating with people who are acting against your convictions. And by having made your decision ahead of time, you don't have to worry about what you will do in such a situation, you'll already know.

Kindness is a language
which the deaf can hear and the blind can see.
-Mark Twain

SOME SNIPPETS TO THINK ABOUT

People can't help but notice you when you step away from the crowd.

If you want to be remembered, *always* be kind, gracious and genuine in your interactions with other people.

You never know, nor should you be concerned with, who is paying attention.

It's not something you should try to fake – people know instinctively when your intentions and behavior aren't genuine.

It costs you nothing to be kind to another human being.

A random smile, a well placed compliment, a kind word are all gifts that cost you nothing, but that have the power to change the recipient's entire day!

One positive encounter with another human being has the potential to change everything. You may never know how your kind words or actions are going to affect another person.

Knowing isn't the point.

Guard well within yourself that treasure, kindness.

Know how to live without hesitation,

how to lose without regret, how to acquire without meanness.

-George Sand

WHAT WILL YOU STAND FOR?

I'm CERTAIN

That it's never too early to take a stand for what you believe.

But

It's probably a good idea to take a moment to figure out what that might be.

How

Do you KNOW what to stand for?

Pay attention to what makes you feel uncomfortable. Notice what boils your blood and ruffles your feathers …

Injustice.
Selfishness.
Poverty.
Violence.
Mean People.
Gossip.
Snobbish Behavior.
Bad Manners.
Bullies.

If you follow your intuition – your gut, you'll figure it out if you pay attention.

SOMETHING JUST ISN'T RIGHT ...

What is this thing called intuition? It could be when your soul whispers a secret to you.

LEARN to recognize when your intuition is trying to tell you something.

PAY ATTENTION! When something just feels off, or not right or a decision you've made or something you're considering doing makes you sick and anxious just thinking about it - That's your intuition warning you ...

DANGER! BAD IDEA! ABORT! STOP! GO BACK! DON'T SAY IT!

HOWEVER, it does work both ways. Intuition is also that warm fuzzy feeling you get when you know you SHOULD do something or GO somewhere or SAY something.

Learn to LISTEN and your intuition won't steer you wrong.

CAN I GET SOME RESPECT?

RESPECT HAS TO BE EARNED. THERE IS NO OTHER WAY TO GET IT.

YOU CAN'T BUY, BORROW OR STEAL IT.

People naturally have respect for a person who stands by her convictions – no matter what. These people come to be known as people we can count on. They're ...

Reliable.

Responsible.

AND ...

Refreshing. Because they are so often a rarity.

JUST IN CASE YOU WERE WONDERING

Being reliable and responsible means that if you say you're going to do something, it gets done. You're on time. You finish what you start. You can be counted on when things get rocky. Your opinion is valued. Your work and your thoughts are respected. You don't do what's popular. You do what's right.

ALWAYS

A rewarding life is full of aspirations such as these …

Striving ALWAYS to …

Be KIND, GRACIOUS and GENUINE.

Show HUMILITY.

TREAT other people like you want to be TREATED.

Assume that EVERYONE MATTERS.

Stick to your CONVICTIONS.

BE TRUE TO YOURSELF.

This above all;
to thine own self be true
and it must follow, as night the day,
thou canst not then be false to any man.
- Shakespeare

RIGHT OR WRONG - OPINIONS MATTER

Allow others to have their opinions – but know that they may not be the same as your own. That's okay. Just because someone has an opinion that's different from yours, doesn't necessarily mean they're wrong and you're right. It only means you see things differently from them.

ALSO ...
It's okay to be wrong.

It really and truly is. We don't always have to be right. No finer person is there than one who can admit when they're wrong. Read that last sentence again, please. It's really important!

FURTHERMORE ...

There is great satisfaction in being right. And it's okay to be right.

BUT ...

There's really no need to rub it in when you ARE right. There is great elegance in being silent and gracious when you have proven someone else to be *incorrect*.

He who knows all the answers

has not been asked all the questions.

-Confucius

LOST IN THE CROWD

Don't let yourself be easily swayed by other people. Stick to your principles and you won't get lost in the crowd of people who may be unaware of where they're being led.

This is huge!

You might find yourself following other people for any number of reasons.

Maybe you like …

THE WAY THEY DRESS,

THE HOUSE THEY LIVE IN,

THE CAR THEY DRIVE,

THE WAY THEY LOOK,

Maybe …

You aren't quite sure where you want to go or who you want to be.

Maybe they told you to follow them.

Whatever reason and whomever you are following, whether it's your neighbor, friend or a celebrity, *give it some thought* as to why you're following them. It's a good idea to ask yourself: Are they going in the RIGHT direction? Do you AGREE with where they're going and what they're doing? Do you agree with how they plan to get there? Do you RESPECT their thoughts and opinions? Do they stand for anything? If you don't consider who you're following you may find yourself in a place you don't want to be. You may find that you followed them right out of a beautiful flower garden and into a bunch of ugly weeds.

It's always best to avoid the weeds!

JUST A THOUGHT ...

It's a good idea to have some idea of where you want to go. Living with intent keeps you from wandering around with no clear idea of where you're going. You can always leave if you don't like it once you get there, but you'll NEVER know unless you make the trip.

If you find a path with no obstacles, it probably

doesn't lead anywhere.

-F. A. Clark

LIVE WITH PURPOSE!

You'll never be a swimmer if you're afraid to get in the water.

If you have a dream of DOING or BEING or SEEING something, then FOCUS your ENERGY on *that* GOAL. Make it your PRIORITY. Figure out what YOU need to do to MAKE IT HAPPEN – and then do whatever that is.

Only YOU stand in the way of your dreams!

So … get out of your own way and get on with it!

STEP AROUND YOUR FEAR AND JUMP RIGHT OVER YOUR SELF DOUBT.

PAY ATTENTION to the things that IGNITE your INTEREST, INTRIGUE your IMAGINATION and figure out what PIQUES your PASSION. Then get moving and PURSUE YOUR PURPOSE.

DON'T WANDER AROUND AIMLESSLY dabbling in whatever diverts your attention and drags you off in the wrong direction –away from your GOAL.

BE A LEADER

EVEN IF YOU'RE ONLY LEADING YOURSELF

Who better to lead you than YOU? A leader becomes a leader by first leading and directing her own life. Others tend to follow when they like the work you've done on yourself.

BUT

Being a leader is not the same as being a bully. Bullies are mean and they thrive on fear.

A true leader DOES NOT DEMAND that others follow. She DOES NOT BECOME ANGRY or upset when things aren't done her way. A great leader just does her thing and sticks to her principles. Others will naturally notice this and follow her example.

THINK ABOUT THIS ...

When you DEMAND that you get your way, you're not being a LEADER, you're either acting selfishly or behaving like a CONTROL FREAK.

If your actions inspire others to dream more,

do more and become more,

you are a leader.

-John Quincy Adams

ASSUME EVERYONE MATTERS

You just <u>never know</u> with whom you're interacting.

AND

That's beside the point. It shouldn't matter anyway.

What could it hurt to aim to treat everyone well?

EVERYONE.

Not just people you think can do something for you AND not just when you know people who can do something for you are watching.

FAMILY TIES

HAVING A PLACE TO GO – IS A HOME. HAVING SOMEONE TO LOVE – IS A FAMILY. HAVING BOTH IS A BLESSING.

-DONNA HEDGES

Never miss out on any OPPORTUNITY to share a meal with your family.

That's SO *In* RIGHT Now!

I can't help noticing that what is popular today is out tomorrow. What was all the rage *then* is now considered ridiculous.

That includes: Fashion * People * Trends * Food * Music * News

And Especially TECHNOLOGY.

Stick to what seems right for you. Hang out with people you genuinely like. Wear the fashion that makes you feel comfortable, listen to the music you enjoy, read the books that make you happy and keep you curious.

Who cares what everyone else is doing!

We don't always need the latest and greatest. It's too much to keep up with, especially in today's fast paced, ever changing world.

Don't spend your life chasing what or whom *the crowd* has deemed popular.

Oh, never mind fashion.

When one has a style of one's own, it is always twenty times better.

-Margaret Oliphant

I've GOT to have it!

We live in an age when unnecessary things are our only necessities.

-Oscar Wilde

When we Want! Want! Want! We will always Need! Need! Need to work longer and harder.

Try ALWAYS to think about the DIFFERENCE between WANT and NEED.

Things (your belongings) taunt you constantly. "Use Me!" Wear Me!" It is stressful to have all that stuff competing for your attention. It's a huge drain on your time to figure out a way to wear all of those shoes, clothes, eye shadow colors and lipstick shades. Just think about that before you start thinking you "NEED" another eye shadow palate or black dress or piece of jewelry. As soon as you take it home, that item is going to be competing with all the other stuff.

The weight of your stuff dragging behind you is a heavy burden to bear.

Live light – live well.

SO MANY BAUBLES TO CHOOSE FROM

Choose a few pieces of jewelry that you love. Wear them and enjoy them. If they break or get lost, at least they weren't hidden away waiting for their turn to go out in public.

The externals are simply so many props; everything we need is within us.

-Etty Hillesum

Which brings me to happiness …

Because I've been known to say (and I know I'm not alone) "This _____ (insert dress, necklace, lipstick, coat, perfume, etc.) is making me so happy right now!" Key words here are *right now.* This feeling that is being associated with happiness doesn't last.

BECAUSE IT ISN'T ABOUT HAPPINESS!

WHAT I KNOW ABOUT HAPPINESS

I know that most people want to be happy. I doubt most people wake up in the morning and say, "I'd like to be miserable today!" But I'm wondering if our culture has bought into the notion that we can't be happy without OWNING or HAVING or BEING certain things.

It's like we chase happiness around a shopping mall, the TV and the Internet. Looking for it in mega sized shoe stores and shiny, sparkly baubles. Thinking we spotted it on a TV series.

Also, we look to other people for our happiness. I wonder if we don't feel entitled to happiness, like we're entitled to free public education. But maybe we have lost our notion of what happiness really is. Thankfully, Helen Keller left us this thought:

What I'm looking for is not out there, it's in me.

When you set your mind to do something worthwhile and you see it through until the end, I promise you this will give you an elated feeling of happiness and fulfillment. But when you rely on people to make you happy, you can be pretty sure they will eventually disappoint you. When you rely on THINGS to make you happy, you will find yourself bogged down with the weight from the bulk of your buying.

THINGS on top of THINGS on top of THINGS!

You can spend all day digging deep into your over-stuffed closet, but I guarantee you won't find any happiness. I know. I've spent days looking for it among all of my stuff.

But I think you might find real joy in doing a hobby or activity that you love.

FIGURE OUT WHAT INTERESTS YOU.
Then do it.

JUST THINK OF all the time you'll have to pursue your
hobby when you aren't buying all that stuff.

STUFF you sometimes have to return.

And while you're there returning it, you buy more STUFF.

STUFF that often doesn't go with anything else in your closet.

So you go shopping to find something that will go with the STUFF.

You have no choice.

And while you're shopping for that, you find a new outfit that simply
can't be left behind.

You must own it.

It would be so cute to wear on a cruise.

Except you aren't planning to go on a cruise.

You buy the outfit.

It's perfect!

Now you have to figure out how you can afford a cruise.

You book the cruise.

Even though you can't afford it.

You can't be happy without going on that cruise.

Except that by the time the cruise rolls around -

you've gained five pounds.

You can't get that outfit zipped.

So you go shopping and …

But I digress …

Just take up painting, photography, running or whatever strikes your fancy.

But know this … shopping is not a hobby.

AND

Things don't make you happy.

If you want others to be happy, practice compassion.
If you want to be happy, practice compassion.
–Dalai Lama

You're better off pursuing KNOWLEDGE and EXPERIENCES than THINGS.

AND …

Having many INTERESTS Makes you a more INTERESTING person.

WHAT'S SO SPECIAL?

Stop saving your belongings to use or wear for a *special occasion.*

Life **_IS_** a special occasion. In fact, it's the main event.

BEAUTY

is not CAUSED.

IT IS.
-Emily Dickinson

GOING THERE IS PART OF GETTING THERE

People in the West are always getting ready to live.

-Chinese Proverb

Always do the best job you can.

People will notice.

This will lead to more opportunities.

More opportunities mean more options.

Having options is wonderful!

If you aren't going to bother doing a job well, then don't bother doing it at all.

Sometimes in life, you have to suck it up and do a job you don't enjoy.

But you still have to do a good job.

IT'S CALLED HAVING A GOOD WORK ETHIC.

A GOOD WORK ETHIC WILL SERVE YOU WELL.

DELIGHT IN YOUR OWN COMPANY

It's better to be alone than in the company of people you don't enjoy.

If you can't stand your own company,
then how is anyone else going to enjoy being with you?

You can be in a room full of a hundred people and still be lonely.

Learn to like yourself. You're pretty much stuck with you.

DEFEND YOUR RELATIONSHIPS

Don't waste your time on relationships that aren't working, especially not a romantic relationship. Maybe the timing isn't right. Maybe the person is flawed … at the moment. Maybe you're flawed … at the moment. You have to fall in love with yourself before you can fall in love with another person. If you don't, you risk being with them for the wrong reasons. Often because you are looking for, in them, what you believe you can't find in yourself. They might not want to give you what you're looking for … it's *something to think about.*

Choose with great care your friends, associates, romantic entanglements, and spouse.

You will be spending your precious time with these people.

Time is not unlimited.

Be certain they are worth your time.

I'll say it again … and this time, I'll underline it.

It is better to be alone than in the company of someone you don't enjoy.

Never allow someone to be your priority

while allowing yourself to be their option.

-Mark Twain

This is so important I'm going to say it AGAIN …

Never allow someone to be your priority
while allowing yourself to be their option.
-Mark Twain

And just in case you have any doubt about how important this is I will go ahead and say it one more time …

Never allow someone to be your priority
while allowing yourself to be their option.
-Mark Twain

Thank you for that gem, Mark Twain.

WHAT'S REALLY IMPORTANT?

GOOD HEALTH.

Truly. If you have your health you have everything. If you don't believe me, just ask someone who is sick – someone who is battling a disease for their life. I bet they would trade all their money and belongings for their health.

He who has health, has hope;

and he who has hope, has everything.

–Thomas Carlyle

Defend your health!

A good place to start is to

THINK ABOUT WHAT YOU'RE EATING!

Did it come out of a box?

Was it developed in a lab?

If it wasn't dug out of the dirt, pulled off a plant, plucked from the ocean, or raised on a farm, it isn't real food.

If you're eating at a franchise place, chances are pretty good it is food that has been processed. How else can it look and taste the same if you were to eat at a chain in New York, New England or New Mexico? Just a little *something to think about.*

E̲AT salad every day.

Our bodies need F̲iber.
We don't get enough of it.

Have fresh FRUIT and V̲egetables every day.

THEY'RE GOOD FOR YOU!

Gummy Fruit snacks are NOT real fruit.

They're sugar or some such variation of sugar and fruit flavored water.

Read the label. You'll see what I'm talking about.

Develop good eating habits now, before the doctor tells you that you have to.

Drink Water
FREQUENTLY throughout the day,
EVERY DAY.

Plants wilt if they don't get enough water. So do people.

Don't forget to water yourself!

Plants and animals don't drink energy drinks and diet sodas. They drink water.

Again ...

Just *something to think about.*

SO MUCH DRAMA!

The Drama will pass.

It always does.

I promise.

The years teach much the days never know.

-Ralph Waldo Emerson

BY THE WAY ...

You only get to be the age you are right now just this once.

Savor it. Own it. Enjoy it.

Each of your moments belongs only to you. Don't thoughtlessly give them away!

JUST BE PRESENT FOR ALL OF YOUR DAYS, THE REST WILL TAKE CARE OF ITSELF.

Fear LESS, Hope MORE;

Whine LESS, breathe MORE;

Talk LESS, say MORE; hate LESS, love MORE;

and all GOOD things are yours.

–Swedish Proverb

Not every second of your life has to be an AMAZING event. I wonder if we don't sometimes try too hard to make everything EPIC. It's a whole lot of pressure. Sometimes it's good just to let things unfold as they will - see where the day takes you.

You just never know what you're going to learn in a seemingly mundane moment in time. You may not even know you were paying attention until years later. Those little nuggets of wisdom are gifts – a delightful surprise that you'll get to open someday in the future.

It's the ordinary moments of our lives that stay with us and come back years later and make us smile. These memories are made up of the smells and sounds and tastes of our lives.

The most treasured moments often happen before or after "the event."

Often, it turns out that they ARE the event.

May you live every day of your life.

-Jonathan Swift

Note that he doesn't say may you simply exist every day of your life. I think to really be alive in one's own life, a person must live with intent and purpose. Wandering around aimlessly is a waste of *your* moments. Interpreting Mr. Swift's quote is certainly *something to think about.*

SORRY!

The sooner you learn the fine art of an apology the better off you'll be.

SORRY!

But a flippant word tossed carelessly at the person does not an apology make. If that's all you can muster, don't bother. An apology needs to be sincere, genuine and heartfelt – otherwise, it doesn't count for much.

Know when you need to say, "I'm sorry."

Own up to mistakes you've made.

Hurtful words you have flung.

Behavior that was hurtful.

Being insensitive.

OWN it. Don't make EXCUSES for it. Don't try to BLAME it on someone or something else.

Just own it. Take responsibility. APOLOGIZE. Get on with your life.

This one humble act is an art to master and is imperative for peace and justice in your life.

WRITE RIGHT

Take time to *write, by hand,* a personal note – even if it's *just because.* One day you will be thrilled to find a snippet of writing from your past.

Texts are LOST with every phone that becomes lost or obsolete.

Email gets LOST amongst spam and with each new computer.

It takes time and effort to sit down with a PEN in hand and a blank sheet of PAPER. It requires time and effort to find a STAMP, address the ENVELOPE and to go to the MAILBOX. But that written piece of correspondence will endure the years and delight the recipient. Not only when they receive it, but also when they find it in a box ten, twenty, thirty years from now.

Fragments of the past will be preserved in the PEN and INK and the POSTMARK. It is a lot of effort, but it sure wouldn't hurt if you took the time to do it every so often.

When you're moved to tell your mom, aunt, third grade teacher or your best friend from childhood how much they mean to you, don't wait a second to do it. Write it down and send it to them. These important sentiments are so much better delivered on an enduring piece of PAPER.

IT'S ABOUT TIME

If I can't say no, then my yes means nothing.

-Anon

BE ON TIME. It's in terribly poor taste to disregard the value of another person's time by being late for an appointed meeting. Of course things come up and circumstances change. But it's a good policy to BE ON TIME.

Don't waste your own TIME doing activities that don't thrill you. Of course there are obligations involving family, school, work and other things that are important. I'm talking about movies, books, music, events and social engagements. The things in that are *optional*. If a book you're reading for pleasure isn't pleasurable then put it down and find one that is.

Don't commit to doing more than you can actually get done without losing your mind. It's okay to say no when people ask you to do something you don't want to do or you don't have TIME to do.

Time is a pretty big deal. When it's gone, it's gone forever!

Defend and Respect it.

Defend your time and have respect for the time of others.

And when you can't do it all, even though you want to, think of this quote courtesy of John Lubbock.

If we are ever in doubt about what to do

it is a good rule to ask ourselves what we shall wish on the morrow

that we had done.

By the way, that goes for making decisions, too.

Forever is composed of nows.
-Emily Dickenson

BORING!

Life is full of so many things to do and be and see that it's difficult to imagine anyone ever saying, "I'm SO BORED!"

BUT just in case, here's a list of possible THINGS for you to DO.

The older you get the more you'll remember fondly the years you seemed to have nothing but time. TIME FLIES (not a time traveling fly) FASTER and FASTER with each passing birthday. You'll see.

The OFFICIAL List
OF THINGS TO DO WHEN
YOU'RE BORED

Write a LETTER

Go for a WALK

Read a BOOK

Ride a BIKE

Bake a CAKE from SCRATCH

Make TAPIOCA PUDDING from SCRATCH

Go back to SCHOOL

Organize your SOCK DRAWER

Start a BOOK CLUB

See how many days it takes you to *Walk* 100,000 STEPS (Make an old-fashioned chart)

Go to the GYM

Plant a GARDEN
Go to a MUSEUM
Get a JOB
Help an ELDERLY NEIGHBOR
Learn a NEW LANGUAGE
Learn to *Play* an INSTRUMENT
Practice YOGA
Braid your SISTER'S HAIR (It's relaxing!)
Cook a SURPRISE DINNER for YOUR PARENTS
Mow the LAWN
Rake LEAVES
Shovel the SIDE-WALK
Make a SNOWMAN
Make a SNOW ANGEL
Volunteer at a SOUP KITCHEN
Watch a SUNSET

Watch a SUNRISE

Take a LUXURIOUS BUBBLE BATH

Color in a COLORING BOOK (Why not?)

Invite your GRANDMA to LUNCH

Host a TEA PARTY for YOUR FRIENDS

Learn to KNIT

Train for a TRIATHLON (I'm serious!)

Go to a PARK and *Swing*

Do SOMETHING NICE for SOMEONE

Surprise your MOM with a CLEAN HOUSE

Take a PAINTING CLASS

Write in a JOURNAL

Run LAPS at a TRACK

Play a GAME of KICK-THE-CAN (YES! It's a real thing, look it up on-line)

Play a GAME of HOPSCOTCH (even if you're 30!)

Play a BOARD GAME with your FAMILY or FRIENDS (you won't be bored.)

Write a STORY *using* these FOUR WORDS: pencil, petunia, perch, pebble

Make a SCRAP BOOK

Make a PHOTO BOOK

Take a SEWING CLASS

Make a LIST of GOALS

Review your LIST of GOALS

Turn off your PHONE for 24 HOURS (I dare you) and *do* TEN THINGS on this LIST.

THINK of THINGS to ADD to this LIST

JUST LISTEN!

Learn to listen to yourself. You are sometimes the only person who has your best interests in mind. If you don't feel right about something *you're doing* or *are going to do*, then DON'T do it. Learn to recognize the difference between something you *shouldn't do* and something you're *afraid to do*.

When someone is talking to you, the courteous thing to do is to listen.

Listening is becoming a lost art.

If you can learn to listen you will be far ahead in your life, your work and your relationships.

There is no higher compliment you can pay to another human being than to actually listen to what they're saying. Give their eyes, your eyes and ...

HEAR their words with your ears

AND

with your heart.

You really hear a person when you take an *authentic* interest in their details.

We have two ears and one mouth so that we can listen

twice as much as we speak.

-Epictetus

HELP!

Learn to ask for help when you need it and offer help when it's needed.

Life would be so much easier for everyone if we lived with this in mind.

Just a little *something to think about.*

Not everything in life requires compensation.

Sometimes you should just help another person and walk away. It is likely they will be so grateful that they will do the same for someone else.

Sometimes random acts of kindness are their own reward.

YOU THINK YOU KNOW EVERYTHING!

The very next time someone older than you offers you their advice maybe just stop for a minute and think about what they have said.

Really. Just consider it.

We all think we know what's best. Maybe sometimes we do. But what can it hurt to examine the advice of someone who has gone before us?

It can't hurt to entertain the idea that we don't know everything.

THINK ABOUT THIS ...

Parents always say, "I just don't want you to make the same mistakes I did." They say this because their parents once told them the very same thing and they know one day you will be telling your own children ... *the exact same thing.*

It bears questioning why NO ONE ever listens.

SO MANY QUESTIONS!

Learn to question things. Not everything is as it seems.

In fact, MOST things aren't. Like …

FOOD INGREDIENTS * PRODUCT CLAIMS * THE NEWS * HISTORY * TV * THE INTERNET

KNOW THIS … Producers of packaged food and retail products have but one goal: To get YOU to buy THEIR products.

But that's not all!

It's pretty hard to find unbiased news reports. BECAUSE …

EVERYONE HAS AN ANGLE

AND

EVERY SPIN CHANGES THE ANGLE.

Just keep these things in mind when hearing, learning, buying or believing – well - most anything.

Question anything that doesn't make sense to you.

Don't be afraid to ask, "Why?"

ALWAYS question anything that sounds too good to be true.

AND … it is absolutely true what they say, whoever they are, "there are always three sides to every story … yours, mine and what really happened."

Wonder is the beginning of wisdom.

-Socrates

SOME MORE THOUGHTS

Don't take yourself too seriously.

People who have learned to laugh at themselves are a delight to be around. I'M SERIOUS.

ALSO

Not everything is about you.

Try not to take every little thing that comes along personally.

People who have the tendency to do this are exhausting to be around.

AND REMEMBER ...

If you can't respect yourself, then how can anyone else respect you?

DEFEND YOUR
CHARACTER, CONVICTIONS,
WORD, WORK ETHIC,
HEALTH,
TIME,
GOALS,
RELATIONSHIPS
AND
anything else you value.

ABOVE ALL ELSE

LOVE, HONOR, RESPECT and DEFEND yourself!

Live your beliefs and you can turn the world around.

-Henry David Thoreau

ONE FINAL, SORT OF RANDOM, THOUGHT...

This is something I REALLY wish I'd been doing my whole life:

SAVING MONEY.

I DARE YOU to SAVE even as little as TEN PERCENT of EVERY SINGLE DOLLAR you earn, starting with your very first job.

If you're already working, then start tomorrow.

I DOUBLE DOG DARE YOU to put that tiny bit of funds into the bank and PRETEND IT ISN'T THERE. I promise you that you'll never miss it.

Otherwise, there's NO question you'll find somewhere to spend it.

It doesn't matter if you're spending or saving – it adds up FAST.

I promise you that you'll never say, "I wish I hadn't saved money!

One day you'll be happy to have something to show for your hard work - besides a closet full of things and a house full of stuff.

Note: I didn't pay attention when my dad suggested this to me when I was young. I sure wish I'd listened … just a little *something to think about.*

HERE'S THE MATH ON THAT:

FOR EVERY DOLLAR YOU EARN THAT'S A MEASLY TEN CENTS. ONE DIME. FOR EVERY TEN DOLLARS YOU EARN THAT'S A BUCK.

DEFEND YOUR DOLLARS!

Beware of little expenses. A small leak will sink a great ship.

–Ben Franklin

P.S. Well, that's pretty much everything I can think of. Oh, I almost forgot. <u>Keep your face, eyes and neck well moisturized.</u> The time to start moisturizing is now. If you wait to see a wrinkle, you're too late. Yep, that's it.

I'm so excited for you as you embark on this phase of your life! You can go out there and be and do anything. I know you'll choose well.

You'll do what you have to do and you'll make mistakes. We all do. It's okay. It's so okay. It's all part of growing-up and no matter what anyone tells you, you will have to decide for yourself. I wish for you a remarkable journey and it's my hope that you live your life in big wide stripes and bold bright colors.

I hope you'll use and enjoy the personal pages included in the back of this book.

You can *write* your own favorite quotes, books you've read and enjoyed, your goals and anything else you might like to leave on the page.

Don't forget to <u>add the date</u> to anything you write.

You'll be glad you have these pages if your computer crashes or your phone gets lost.

THE PERSONAL PAGES OF

_____

MY PERSONAL COLLECTION OF QUOTES

MY PERSONAL COLLECTION OF QUOTES

MY PERSONAL COLLECTION OF QUOTES

MY FAVORITE BOOKS

MY GOALS FOR THIS YEAR

MY GOALS FOR THE NEXT FIVE YEARS

MY GOALS FOR THE NEXT TEN YEARS

MY THOUGHTS

MY THOUGHTS

MY FAVORITE MEMORIES

I Remember when ...

_____
_____
_____
_____
_____
_____
_____
_____
_____
_____
_____
_____
_____
_____
_____
_____
_____
_____
_____
_____
_____
_____
_____

A LIST OF MY FAVORITE WORDS

A LETTER TO MY OLDER SELF

DEAR,

_____

_____

_____

_____

_____

_____

_____

_____

_____

_____

_____

_____

_____

_____

_____

_____

_____

_____

_____

_____

_____

_____

_____

_____

_____

_____

_____

_____

_____

A LETTER TO MY BEST FRIEND FROM ELEMENTARY SCHOOL

DEAR,

_____

_____

_____

_____

_____

_____

_____

_____

_____

_____

_____

_____

_____

_____

_____

_____

_____

_____

_____

_____

_____

_____

_____

_____

_____

_____

_____

A LETTER OF THANKS TO SOMEONE WHO MADE A DIFFERENCE IN MY LIFE

DEAR,

_____

_____

_____

_____

_____

_____

_____

_____

_____

_____

_____

_____

_____

_____

_____

_____

_____

_____

_____

_____

_____

_____

_____

_____

_____

_____

_____

_____

A LETTER TO MY CHILDHOOD HOME

DEAR,

_____
_____
_____
_____
_____
_____
_____
_____
_____
_____
_____
_____
_____
_____
_____
_____
_____
_____
_____
_____
_____
_____
_____
_____
_____
_____

A LETTER TO MY FIRST PAIR OF HIGH HEEL SHOES

DEAR,

_____

_____

_____

_____

_____

_____

_____

_____

_____

_____

_____

_____

_____

_____

_____

_____

_____

_____

_____

_____

_____

_____

_____

_____

_____

_____

_____

_____

_____

PLACES I'VE BEEN

PLACES I WANT TO SEE

MY FAVORITE SONGS

Aunt Kimmie lives in Spokane, Washington with her husband. She believes in sending handwritten notes of thanks, random acts of kindness, and that good manners never go out of style.

She is also the author of two children's books, *Magic Sprinkles* and *The Goosie's New Pond.*

Made in the USA
Middletown, DE
05 October 2015